ETHICS

CHRISTIAN

This booklet is copyright and may not be copied or reproduced, in whole or part, by any means, without the publisher's prior written consent.

© Copyright 2003
First published 2003

Abacus Educational Services
424 Birmingham Road
Marlbrook
Bromsgrove
Worcestershire
B61 0HL

ISBN 1 898653 25 9

Other titles available in this series:
1. Ethical Theory and Language
2. Moral Rules
4. Homosexuality
5. Abortion
6. Euthanasia
7 Environmental Ethics

Also available:

Philosophy of Religion series:
1. Religious Language
2. The Problem of Evil
3. Faith and Reason
4. God and Proof
5. Revelation and Religious Experience
6. Life after Death
7. Miracles
8. Science and Religion
9. Freewill and Determinism

Other titles on Philosophy, Synoptic Gospels and Fourth Gospel are also available.

CONTENTS

INTRODUCTION	4
WHAT IS DISTINCTIVE ABOUT CHRISTIAN ETHICS?	5
WHAT CAN THE NEW TESTAMENT CONTRIBUTE TO ETHICS?	15
CAN CHRISTIAN ETHICS BE BASED ON THE BIBLE?	23
ARE CHRISTIAN ETHICS RELEVANT TO MODERN SOCIETY?	29
REFERENCES	33
WORKSHEET	34
EXAM QUESTION	35
FURTHER READING	37

INTRODUCTION

This booklet has been written specifically to cater for the needs of A2/AS students of Philosophy and Religious Studies. However, it may equally be used as an introduction to ethics by the interested lay person or by first year undergraduates.

The booklet is similar in style to that employed in other booklets in other series. It is structured around key questions that have developed from classroom experience. It also contains a section that deals with exam questions and should therefore be useful for both teaching and revision.

Philosophy, of which ethics is a part, can be great fun to both study and to teach. It is a subject that both staff and students can become fully engaged in. It is therefore hoped that learning about ethics will prove to be an enjoyable experience.

WHAT IS DISTINCTIVE ABOUT CHRISTIAN ETHICS?

▶ THE NATURE OF ETHICS.

In the first booklet of this series, entitled 'Ethical Theory and Language', John Lee outlined the nature of ethics. He distinguished between **metaethics**, which is concerned with the nature of the language used in talking about ethics, **normative ethics**, which discusses whether there are rules determining what is right or wrong and **practical ethics**, which describes how ethics can be applied to specific situations. In discussing the meaning of ethical terms he pointed out that moral terms can be either **objective**, that is true for everyone, or **subjective** and therefore dependent on the beliefs and feelings of the person experiencing them. Lee also pointed out that ethics can be looked upon as **absolute**, that is true in all situations or **relative** and hence dependent on changing circumstances. Examples of absolute ethical theories are **deontology**, which is concerned with duties binding upon everyone and **naturalism**, which claims that we can know what is right by observing nature. Relative morality finds expression in **hedonism**, which claims that what is right is what brings the individual pleasure. **Utilitarianism** is an extension of hedonism. It is concerned to discover what brings happiness or pleasure to the greatest number of people. The crucial issue in ethical theory, which Lee addresses in the last chapter of his booklet, is why we should act morally.

▶ BELIEF IN GOD AS THE BASIS FOR ETHICS.

Much of modern ethical theory has no time for religious questions and sees the existence of God as irrelevant in discussing morality. The rejection of God as the ultimate lawgiver raises questions about the nature of moral obligation and the notion of right and wrong. This was recognised by Professor Anscombe in her seminal essay in 1958, entitled 'Modern Moral Philosophy', in which she argued that modern ethical philosophy needs to find a new justification for morality. She pointed out that, "To have a *law* conception of ethics is to hold that what is needed for conformity with the virtues failure which is the mark of being (a) bad man...is (a belief in)...divine law. Naturally it is not possible to have such a conception unless you believe in God as a law giver; like Jews, Stoics and Christians."[1]

▶PRESUPPOSITIONS OF CHRISTIAN ETHICS.

Christian ethics take the existence of God as the starting point for ethical discussion. A belief in God alone is not sufficient for ethics. A person can believe in God as necessary for the existence of the universe and all that is in it, as a number of scientists do, without believing God to be a moral being or to have anything to do with the world that he created. For God to be the basis for morality it is necessary to believe that God is a moral being and that we can know what God commands to be right. Technically God's communication is known as revelation, which takes two forms. General revelation is available to everybody, but special revelation is God's specific revelation to particular individuals. Naturalism is an aspect of general revelation as is virtue ethics and the belief in a conscience. Christians believe that God revealed his requirements for living the good life to prophets and teachers. Moses, for example, was both a lawgiver and a prophet. For Christians the primary source of God's revelation is Jesus, who, in the Fourth Gospel, is called the 'Word of God'. Paul and other writers in the New Testament seek to interpret and apply the teaching of Jesus to the situation of their own day. Many Christians believe that the words of these teachers and what they mean and how they should be applied has been recorded in the Bible. Other Christians, especially Roman Catholics, believe that God has spoken and continues to speak through the Church and especially through church leaders, like the Pope, who have a role in interpreting God's commands and applying them to changing circumstances. The Roman Catholic Church has tended to use a variety of sources for Christian ethics, including the Bible, Christian tradition, human reason and the teaching of the Church. Protestantism, by contrast, has put major emphasis on the Bible. The catch phrase of the Reformation was *'Sola fide, sola gratia, sola Scriptura'* (Faith alone, grace alone and Scripture alone.) Although in the past the existence of God as a law giver and the supreme authority of the Bible, and in some cases, the authority of the church or church leaders, were taken for granted, this is no longer the case.

▶ DEONTOLOGY AND THE EUTHYPHRO DILEMMA.

The Greek philosopher Plato (428-347 BC), in his Euthyphro Dialogue, asked the question, "Is what is holy, holy because the gods approve of it, or do they approve of it because it is holy?" In other words do we obey God's commands because they are good or because God tells us to obey them?

The dilemma can be put in this way:

(a) If God commands or approves an action because it is right, then the action is right irrespective of whether or not God approves of it.

(b) If the action is right because God commands it, then any action that God commands must be right. Morality then becomes obedience to God.

(c) If (a) is right then morality is independent of God and God is no longer supreme. If (b) is right then any action that God commands, like murder and adultery, become good by definition.

Most Christian moralists would say that God is perfect and would only command what is right, but there have been some, who would agree with (c) that whatever God commands is right. For instance, Duns Scotus (1266-1308) believed that God was free to command fornication, human sacrifice and other supposed immoral acts and we would be obliged to do them. William of Ockham (1285-1347) went further and said that God could even have commanded us to hate our neighbours or even God himself and we would be duty bound to obey him.

The belief that Christian morality consists in obedience to an external authority, like God, or to the dictates of conscience or a sense of duty are examples of absolute morality. Immanuel Kant (1724-1804) did not believe that God's existence could be proved rationally but argued that in order for mankind to act morally there had to be a perfect God. Kant was a deontologist, that is he believed that individuals have a duty or obligation to seek the highest good. However, although the highest good must be possible to attain to, in actual fact human beings do not attain to it in this life. Therefore, he argues, there must be a God who makes this possible and an afterlife in which it can be attained. Interestingly Kant did not believe that moral duty consists in obedience to God's commands. Moral acts must be free actions undertaken without any external pressure. If we act morally because God tells us to or to avoid punishment or to receive a reward then the act is done for ulterior motives. By its very nature deontology is absolute. To declare something to be wrong is not to give reasons. Murder is not wrong because God says it is, or because the law of the land forbids it. It is simply wrong. Kant called this a categorical imperative. We must always do what is right because it is right and we have a permanent duty to do what is right.

▶OBEDIENCE TO GOD'S COMMANDMENTS AND CHRISTIAN ETHICS.

An example of regarding ethics as a form of obedience is found in the Jewish attitude to the Bible. For Jews the heart of the Bible is the *Torah*, a Hebrew word which means law, direction or instruction. The Torah consists of the first five books of the Bible, even though not all of these books consist entirely of laws. For Jewish people the Bible essentially reveals God's guidance for regulating every aspect of daily life. However, as the Torah only deals with a limited area of life it became necessary to expand the Biblical laws so that they could be applied to every circumstance that arose and would arise in the future. It was the job of teachers (*rabbis*) to interpret the law. At first the teaching was handed down by word of mouth (the oral tradition that Jesus often criticised), but eventually it was written down between the third and ninth centuries AD and is known as the *Mishna* (repetition) and the *Talmud* (studying). Jewish people are divided as to whether the oral law has the same authority as the written law. Orthodox Jews generally believe that, like the written law, the oral law was passed down from Moses and the prophets.

The problem of the Orthodox Jewish approach for Christian ethics is that the laws do not easily transfer to modern society. This is implicit in the formation of the Talmud, which saw the necessity to interpret and apply the laws to changing circumstances. Some Old Testament laws and punishments are illegal in modern society, for instance capital punishment for kidnapping, striking parents, apostasy and various sexual offences including adultery and homosexuality. One obvious response is that Christian Ethics are meant to challenge social ethics not to simply conform to them. This was the view of the Protestant reformer Martin Bucer (1491-1551), who believed that the kings of England should regulate the life of the nation under the guidance of the Old Testament and have the death penalty for blasphemy, adultery, rape and Sabbath violation. A similar position is taken by a group of modern Christians called reconstructionists. An example of how this is applied in practice can be seen in the Islamic states that have re-establish Shariah law as the basis for their ethics.

Also it is impossible to treat all the laws equally. For instance it is sometimes necessary to make a choice between apparently categorical requirements. In the Ten Commandments God requires both absolute truth and refraining from murder. If you were sheltering someone from a murderer would you betray him to his assailant because you would otherwise be telling a lie? The Torah itself gives examples of God's approving of lying where the taking of innocent lives was involved. The midwives in Egypt lied rather than carry out the pharaoh's command to kill the Hebrew boys. (Exodus 1:15-20).

▶ **THE OLD TESTAMENT LAW IN CONTEXT.**

The modern Jewish understanding of Torah represents how things were after the Jewish nation had been forced into exile and had to leave behind all the traditional trappings of their religion which was based around the Temple and a priesthood. In exile new meeting places (synagogues) were established and obedience to the law became the essential ingredient for keeping Jewish national identity.

Originally the Torah was seen as a covenant (a binding agreement) between God and his people, Israel. The idea of covenant went back to the time of Noah and Abraham, but was modelled on Vassal Treaties, which were made between great kingdoms and smaller dependent nations from the time of Abraham onwards. These treaties open with a list of the suzerain's (the great king of the superior nation) titles and a list of his mercies and acts of kindness to the subject nation. The major section of the document outlined the duties of the vassal (subject nation), which were to be faithful at all times, to assist in battle and to pay tribute. The final section told of blessing that would result from obedience and curses that would come upon the nations in the event of disobedience. The law codes in the Torah follow this pattern. God is the great king, to whom the king, priests, prophets and people were subjects. Obedience to the law was out of gratitude for what God had done for them in choosing them to be his special people, bringing them out of slavery in Egypt and giving them a land and prosperity. There is an emphasis throughout on treating people fairly and protecting the weak and vulnerable. This is summed up in Deuteronomy 10:17-20.

"For the Lord your God is God of gods and Lord of lords, the great God, mighty and awesome, who shows no partiality and accepts no bribes. He defends the cause of the fatherless and the widow, and loves the alien, giving him food and clothing. And you are to love those who are aliens, for you yourselves were aliens in Egypt. Fear the Lord your God and serve him."

The Torah law was not thought of as oppressive, but rather as something that would enable them to prosper and live a good life. Much of the Wisdom Literature in the Old Testament extolled the law as something to be loved and to be grateful for. (See especially Psalm 119, which is a song in praise of the Law). This idea of ethics being based on a loving response to God's grace is developed in more detail in the teaching of the New Testament. It is based on a society that is ruled over by God (a theocracy) and it is at odds with our idea of liberal democracy.

▶THE LAW WITHIN - A UNIVERSAL MORALITY?

In the ancient world generally religion and morality were not separate issues, although ethical ideals varied considerably between different nations. Faced with the prospect of addressing a pagan society Paul, the Jewish Christian apostle to the non-Jews, needed to explain how the one true God treated those who were unacquainted with Torah. This he does by appealing to general revelation. In writing to the church in Rome he says,

> "The wrath of God is being revealed from heaven against all the godlessness and wickedness of men who suppress the truth by

their wickedness, since what may be known about God is plain to them ... For since the creation of the world God's invisible qualities-his eternal power and divine nature-have been clearly seen, being understood from what has been made, so that men are without excuse." (Romans 1:18-20)

He explains how the non-Jews (Gentiles) know what is right: -

"Indeed, when Gentiles, who do not have the law, do by nature things required by the law, they are a law to themselves, even though they do not have the law, since they show that the requirements of the law are written on their hearts, their consciences also bearing witness, and their thoughts now accusing, now even defending them." (Romans 2:14-15)

▶CHRISTIAN ETHICS AND NATURAL LAW.

Commentators disagree among themselves as to what exactly Paul means by 'doing by nature things required by the law' and whether or not the phrase incorporates the philosophical ideas, both Roman and Greek, of his own time. In the history of Christian thought 'doing by nature the things required by the law' has been used as a basis for the idea of natural law. Plato believed that goodness consisted not of thoughtless conformity to social conventions but of living in accordance with ones rational nature. The Roman statesman and moralist, Marcus Cicero (106-43 BC) wrote that, "True law is right reason in agreement with Nature; it is of universal application, unchanging and everlasting; it summons to duty by its commands and averts from wrongdoing by its prohibitions" {De.Republica.3.28, 33-34)

The most important exponent of natural law in the ancient world was Aristotle (384-322 BC), whose ideas were adapted for Christianity by the influential medieval philosopher-theologian Thomas Aquinas (1224-1274). Aristotle argued that what is meant by 'good' is whatever fulfils the purpose for which it has been made. Thus a good knife is one that cuts well. Aquinas uses "good" in terms of things and people fulfilling the end for which God had created them. He distinguished between potentiality and actuality. A 'potential' person is an embryo, a potential oak tree is an acorn. The more the potentiality that is realised the better the thing or person. For him a healthy, educated man with a clear conscience was better than an ignorant and vicious one. How do we find out what is right? Aquinas said we do this by observing the world and human nature, by the revelation of God's purposes in the Bible and through the teaching of the Church. He adopted a hierarchy of levels of morality. Each level is related to the one above it. The levels were:

(a) Eternal - order in the mind of God, which is absolute and enables us to judge between conflicting moralities.

(b) Divine - God's law mediated through special revelation - the Bible and the Church. This needed the combination of faith and reason.

(c) Natural - the inborn sense of right and wrong (conscience). He believed that children have an inborn sense of fairness.

(d) Human - the rules created by society to enable it to work.

The teaching of Thomas Aquinas has been particularly influential in the Roman Catholic Church and is reflected in Papal Encyclicals, which are the authoritative teachings that Catholics are expected to obey. A recent example of such teaching is the encyclical *Humanae vitae* issued by Pope Paul VI in 1986. In this he said that since procreation is the natural purpose of sexual intercourse then all efforts to prevent procreation (birth control, masturbation, abortion, homosexuality) are 'intrinsically evil'. Neither good motives nor perceived bad consequences, like the escalating world population, can justify the deliberate violation of what is considered to be the divine natural order.

▶ THE INADEQUACY OF THE NATURAL LAW ARGUMENT FOR CHRISTIAN ETHICS

(a) Aquinas' natural law argument assumes not only the existence of God but also that there is an agreement about what is 'natural', which is not the case.

(b) If natural law is strictly applied then it becomes contradictory. If natural law teaches that the purpose of existing as male and female is to reproduce then how could Aquinas justify the teaching of his church that he, as a priest, should remain celibate? He replied that as long as humanity as a whole fulfilled the purpose then exceptions could be accepted. If this is so then why should not homosexuals, who according to the natural law argument are unnatural, be exceptions? Does it not also encourage injustice by allowing some people to be exempt from the rules they impose on others?

(c) Aquinas was too optimistic in his view of human nature and the limits of reason. Not everybody has the same rational ability, nor is everyone inclined towards goodness.

(d) Aquinas believed that immorality is a mistaken belief on the part of the wrongdoer believing he was doing the right thing. This is not always the case. Some people choose to do what they know to be wrong and others do evil deliberately to gain notoriety.

(e) The Bible teaches about man's fallen nature and its effect upon the ability to know and do what is right. Many Christian critics feel that Aquinas, and others who argue for natural law, fail to take this aspect of Bible teaching seriously enough.

(f) This teaching commits the naturalistic fallacy. That is it assumes that you can translate matters of fact into value judgements. Just because the human sexual organs are primarily designed for reproduction it does not mean that they cannot be used to give pleasure without procreation. Similarly, because evolution demonstrates that only the fittest survive, this does not mean that we have a duty to destroy infants, who are born with disabilities.

▶ THE LAW WITHIN - CONSCIENCE.

The word 'conscience' means literally 'knowing together with' and is therefore more than an individual judgement. Conscience is shaped within the community. It is not merely a personal preference, but is the ability to understand general moral principles as well as the ability to apply these principles to particular situations. The Bible employs the term to both a good and bad conscience. A good conscience attests a person's integrity and a bad conscience causes him to experience reproach. The Roman Catholic document *Gaudium et Spes* describes conscience as, "...a law which (a man) does not impose upon himself, but which holds him to obedience ... For man has in his heart a law written by God ... Conscience is the most secret core and sanctuary of a man. There he is alone with God, whose voice echoes in his depths." Even though Christians have claimed that conscience is the voice of God within, conscience is not infallible. It is the capacity for hearing God's voice, which must be judged and educated by the Bible and experience. Some would also include the 'magesterium' (the Pope and Bishops), which Roman Catholics believe are guided by the Holy Spirit or the advice of mature Christians. Conscience can err through ignorance of all the facts or through distortion. Even when someone sincerely desires to do what is right she can still be in error. An informed conscience requires both the possession and appreciation of moral values and also the awareness of ones strengths and weaknesses. Conscience cannot be the primary decider for Christian ethics. It is not the alternative to obeying external rules. It is not a licence to do what we want but the freedom to do what is right. This still leaves the question of how we know what is right and how we are able to do what is right. These are two major issues addressed by the New Testament.

WHAT CAN THE NEW TESTAMENT CONTRIBUTE TO ETHICS?

▶THE BIBLE AND ETHICS.

It is often assumed in books about Christian ethics that one can extract ethical teaching from the Bible and apply it directly to moral issues. This is not the case. Even if one believes that all the ethical teaching recorded in the Bible is exactly what was originally said, and there are many biblical scholars who do not believe this, it is still necessary to know the original context and whether what was said at that time is applicable to a very different situation now. Gareth Jones points to five significant questions that need to be answered, before we can discover what contribution the Bible can make to Christian ethics [2]. These questions are:

(a) What Bible texts are used?

(b) How does the author of those texts use Scripture?

(c) How authoritative is the Bible?

(d) What method of interpretation is used?

(e) What is the relationship between the Bible text and Christian ethics?

The first two of these questions will concern us in this chapter, which deals primarily with what the Jesus is reported to have said and how Jesus' teaching was understood and applied by Paul and the other writers in the New Testament. The other three will be the subject of the next chapter.

▶THE TEACHING OF JESUS - TEXT AND CONTEXT.

Unlike the Torah, which consists of detailed codes of law, which can be applied to different moral issues, there is no systematic moral teaching in the Gospels. Even the 'Sermon on the Mount' is probably a collection of Jesus' teaching given on several occasions and put together by the author. This is brought out by the fact that many of the sayings in Matthew's version of the sermon are found in different contexts in Luke's gospel. Also much of Jesus' teaching is given in the form of parables, which are not always capable of a simple explanation, but may be open to multiple interpretations. Even apparently clear teaching on subjects like divorce cannot be simply lifted from the text as the authoritative teaching of Jesus without an understanding of what Jesus assumed his hearers already accepted as given. Thus to maintain that Jesus taught that divorce could only be granted on the ground of 'indecency' (even the meaning of this word- *porneia* in Greek-is open to various interpretations) fails to take account of the context. The grounds for divorce in Judaism at the time of Jesus, based on the interpretation of Old Testament law, were adultery, physical and emotional abuse and, in some cases, infertility. It is likely, but not certain, that Jesus would have accepted some, or all of these reasons.

▶JESUS THE JEW.

Jesus was born and brought up as a Jew and accepted the Old Testament as the word of God. He maintained that he had not come to abolish the law and the prophets and that his disciples must keep the law also. He said, " ... until heaven and earth disappear, not the smallest letter, not the least stroke of a pen, will by any means disappear from the Law until everything is accomplished. Anyone who breaks one of the least of these commandments and teaches others to do the same will be called least in the kingdom of heaven." (Matthew 5:18-19). As was pointed out earlier, after the Jewish nation lost its Temple and was expelled from its own land, Jewish teachers had added to the laws of Moses. By the time of Jesus many Jews had returned to Israel and the Temple had been rebuilt. The Jewish nation was also now ruled by the Romans. The centre of the Jewish religion continued to be the synagogue and the Pharisees and the Scribes (legal experts) were seen as the guardians and expositors of the law. Jesus was closest to the Pharisees, who were godly layman, and had friends among them who invited him to meals, and some, like Nicodemus, became very interested in Jesus' teaching. Nevertheless his strongest criticisms were directed at the Pharisees and Scribes who wanted to apply the laws to every area of life and to 'put a fence round the Torah'. The other group, with whom Jesus had little in common, was the Sadducees, an aristocratic group, consisting of the priests and the ruling class within the Jewish Council. They were pro-Roman and were considered to be corrupt in their administration of the temple. One particular scandal at the time of Jesus was the policy to move money changers into the Temple Court. No doubt Jesus' expulsion of the money changers (Mark 11:15-18) gave him considerable popular support.

The Jewish scholar Joseph Klausner, who took a particular interest in Christianity, claimed that Jesus' teaching was not original. He declared that, " ...throughout the gospels there is not one item of ethical teaching which cannot be paralleled either in the Old Testament, the Apocrypha, or in the Talmudic or Midrashic literature of the period near to the time of Jesus."[3] Jesus did not claim originality but rather that he was bringing out the full significance of the law of Moses. Nevertheless it seems improbable that Jesus would have been conversant with all this literature, some of which was not written down until much later. Where Klausner and also Christian scholars have seen Jesus' originality is in bringing together all of this moral teaching into a coherent whole and in his uncompromising attitude. Klausner believes that Jesus was guilty of over-emphasising ethics in contrast to the teaching of Judaism, which offers a practical and theological basis for every aspect of daily life. Colin Hart comments on this. " It is possible to acknowledge the accuracy of Klausner's description of Jesus' ethics without sharing his evaluation of it. Jesus does, indeed, seem more concerned about principles than their practical implications and about absolutes rather than the compromises and hard choices of everyday life, but I see that as a strength, not a weakness."[4] Similarly Donald Macleod writes, " ... Christians should not be embarrassed by claims that there is little originality in the teaching of Jesus. He specifically disclaimed such originality. His uniqueness lay in more challenging areas: in his identity as the eternal Son, in the redemptive object of his mission (to give his life a ransom for many, Mark 10:45), and in his projection of himself as not merely a devout worshipper but as the worshipped one. He is not a rival Moses, but Moses' Lord. (Heb.3:5-6)" [5]

▶JESUS AND THE MORAL LAW.

Jesus accepted the Old Testament as the word of God and in his discussion with the lawyers would refer them back to it. For instance when asked whether it was permissible for a man to divorce his wife for any reason, he referred them back to a higher law, the creation ordinance of Gen. 2:24, and said that divorce was a concession to man's sin and was not God's original intention. When he was asked, by the Pharisees, what the greatest commandment was, he referred his questioner back to the Torah: love God with all your heart (Deut. 6:5) and love your neighbour as yourself (Lev. 19:18). "All the Law and the Prophets", he said, "hang on these two commandments." (Mt. 22:40) The Pharisees would have agreed with the answer because an almost identical statement occurs in the Mishna.

If Jesus and the Pharisees had so much in common why did he criticise them so vehemently? There are a number of reasons:

- (a) Legalism tends to lead to pride and self-righteousness. Many of the Pharisees were self-righteous. Jesus taught that the moral person was humble and concerned for others.

- (b) The Pharisees concentrated on the implementation of the law irrespective of how much suffering was caused in applying it.

- (c) For the ordinary person many of the petty regulations in the oral law were impractical, too costly and often not even known to them. Jesus claimed, "They tie up heavy loads and put them on men's shoulders, but they themselves are not willing to lift a finger to move them." (Mt. 23:2)

- (d) The law could only deal with externals and could easily lead to hypocrisy with people obeying the words of the law but ignoring the spirit. Jesus, especially in the 'Sermon on the Mount' emphasised the importance of motives.

- (e) This led to inconsistency. The Pharisee could parade his outward conformity to the law while at the same time oppressing the poor or using one law to undermine another, for instance by making an oath to devote his money to God when he should be supporting his parents with it (Mk. 7:9-13).

- (f) The Pharisees became exclusivists and despised everyone who was not a Jew. Jesus shocked his contemporaries with his caring attitude to women, outcasts and the enemies of the Jews - the Samaritans and the Romans. He taught that we should love our enemies and illustrated what this love meant by telling the parable of the Good Samaritan.

(g) Jesus accused them of concentrating on the minutiae at the expense of the important. He said, "You give a tenth of your spices (to God)... But have neglected the more important matters of the law - justice, mercy and faithfulness. You should have practised the latter without neglecting the former. You blind guides! You strain out a gnat but swallow a camel." (Mt. 23:23-24)

Lest we should think that Jesus was being unnecessarily hostile towards a respected group of leaders, it is important to realise that the Mishna and Talmud admits that there were more bad types of Pharisee than good ones.

R.E.O.White summarises Jesus' ethical teaching in these words, "Whenever ritual and ethical ordinances are placed on the same level and enforced with the same degree of authority, the moral sense becomes confused between the really important and the plainly trivial: ritualist reasons can be given for moral barbarities (like stoning for adultery); and religious explanations can be given for evading the clearest moral duties, as the priest and levite ignore the stricken traveller by the roadside. In all such cases Jesus stated the plain deliverance of the enlightened conscience: the sabbath was made for man; compassion must rule ones actions on the sabbath as on every day; what comes out of a man's heart defiles him, not what goes into his stomach; loyalty to needy parents is far more important than scruples about ill tempered vows." [6]

▶ PERSONAL AND SOCIAL ETHICS.

Jesus saw himself as inaugurating the Kingdom (or reign) of God on earth and his followers were to be citizens of that kingdom and their lives should be an example to others. Their first duty was to God, which was the point of Jesus' enigmatic reply to the question about giving taxes to Caesar (Mark 12:13-17) in which Jesus reminded them to "give to God what is God's". His followers were to be lights in a dark world just as he was the 'Light of the World'. Consequently much of the ethical teaching in the Gospels is about how a Christian should live rather than comments on what governments should do. It is important to remember this when interpreting Jesus' teaching about non-violence. His teaching, "Do not resist an evil person. If someone strikes you on the right cheek turn to him the other also." (Mt.5:39) has led some Christians to assume that Jesus advocated pacifism or even that any violence against another person, such as a murderer, cannot be condoned. Actually Jesus said nothing about the penalty for murder and, therefore, by implication, it might be argued that he accepted the right of the government to impose what they considered the appropriate punishment. As individuals, Christians should be prepared to be wronged rather than hold out for their rights. Paul later applied this to Christians taking one another to secular courts. (1 Corinthians 6:1-8) The teaching on non-retaliation cannot be forced on others. White comments, "This does not touch the wider question of the Christian reaction to evil in society, as it bears upon *other* individuals and infects the common life ... the ordinary processes of law, justice and government, by which society is disciplined and crime restrained and punished, Jesus accepted without question." [7]

▶LIVING AS THE PEOPLE OF GOD - THE NEW TESTAMENT LETTERS.

When we turn to the rest of the New Testament for guidance about Christian ethics we find the same problem that we did in the Gospels. The writers of the letters to the newly formed Christian churches were addressing specific issues as they arose. Whenever possible, the writers would appeal to the teaching of Jesus, which had yet to be written down. When this was not possible they would give their own opinion, guided by the Holy Spirit. For instance Paul had no teaching from Jesus about virgins but said, " ...I give a judgement as one who by the Lord's mercy is trustworthy." (1 Cor. 7:25) There is an added complication in that only one side of a dialogue has survived. We often do not know what the situation was that is being addressed nor whether what Paul says in, for instance, his letter to the Corinthian Church, consist of quotations from his correspondents or whether he is using his own words.

▶THE LAW AND FREEDOM.

Jesus had stated that the goal of the Christian life was that his followers should be perfect as God was perfect. (Matthew 5:48) This echoes the demand of the Old Covenant in the Torah; "I am the Lord who brought you up out of Egypt to be your God, therefore be holy, because I am holy." (Leviticus 11:40) The same theme recurs in Peter's first letter; "for it is written, 'Be holy, because I am holy.'" (1:16). How is this holiness to be achieved? It was recognised by the Jews of Jesus' day that it was impossible to achieve salvation by keeping the law. Paul emphasised this point repeatedly. The Law was compared to a schoolmaster (Greek *paidagōgos* - the Roman slave employed to instruct and discipline a child until he was mature - Galatians 3:24). When the child became an adult the slave was no longer necessary. It was the same with the Jewish Law. For Christians, the law was regarded as the Jewish response to God's covenant, which was fulfilled in Christ. Jesus had himself claimed to fulfil the Law. The law brought knowledge of wrongdoing but was unable to make a person perfect. There was a new way of achieving righteousness through faith in Jesus Christ. This had to be worked out in practice. The Christian must co-operate with God in order to achieve holiness. This involves the will in resisting temptation and in abstaining from sinful desires, the mind by taking every thought captive and the body (the temple of the Holy Spirit) by not indulging in immoral acts.

Jesus had emphasised the importance of his followers setting an example in morality and this was the theme in the rest of the New Testament. In the description of the beginnings of the early church the believers had everything in common and sold possessions to give to the needy, which in turn brought commendation from those outside their number. (Acts.2:42-47) The motive for Christian ethics was to be love for others. The failure to show such love elicited the corrective moral teaching we find in Paul's letters. Paul also gave us the magnificent exposition of love in a letter addressed to a failing church (1 Corinthians 13). In stressing the importance of communal sharing and caring for the underprivileged, both Jesus and the other New Testament writers reflected the beliefs of both Jews and Gentiles of that time. In Judaism giving to the poor was one of the three primary acts of devotion. The others were prayer and fasting. Jesus commented on all three in the Sermon on the Mount (Mt. 6:1-17). For the Romans the path to power was to keep the masses happy and well fed.

▶ LIBERTY AND LIBERTARIANISM.

Paul clearly saw the implications of the teaching of Jesus about love in the breaking down of barriers between men and women, rich and poor, citizens and slaves . There could no longer be an exclusivism of the kind he had practised as a Pharisee. "There is," he said, "neither Jew nor Greek, slave nor free, male nor female, for you are all one in Christ Jesus." (Gal. 3:28). How was this to be worked out in practice? Unlike our society, which stresses the rights of the individual, the society of his day was centred around the extended family or 'household', which in richer families consisted not only of parents and children, but also of slaves. The later New Testament letters give specific instructions regarding the outworking of Christian ethics within the family groups (for example see Col. 3:18–4:1; Eph.5:22–6:9). In these passages the duties and responsibilities of each group are clearly stated, but with the added obligation of doing everything out of love. Christians must always remember that they have a Master in heaven, to whom they are responsible. The authority structure of these passages has been criticised and condemned by modern Christians as being oppressive and unacceptable for us today. This will be one of the issues addressed in the next section.

CAN CHRISTIAN ETHICS BE BASED ON THE BIBLE?

▶ THE TRADITIONAL VIEW OF THE BIBLE.

Until about the 17th Century AD (the time of the Enlightenment) the Christian Church accepted that the Bible was the Word of God and the supreme authority for faith and practice. There was a long debate about the content of the Bible and the Roman Catholic Church accepted additional books (the Apocrypha), which were rejected by the Protestant Church. For the most part, Christian leaders and teachers accepted that the way to interpret the Bible was the application of the historical-critical method, which seeks to find the meaning of the text by investigating the original intention of the writer and by the use of critical reason to apply it to the reader's situation. Some of the Christian leaders of the early centuries of the Christian era, the Church Fathers, applied allegory in their attempt to understand and apply certain teaching about ethics but this was always regarded as secondary to the literal meaning. Gerald Bray quotes Augustine, " As well as the rule, which warns us not to pursue a figurative expression as if it were literal, we must add a further one: not to accept a literal one as if it were figurative. Generally speaking it is this: anything in the divine discourse that cannot be related either to good morals or to the true faith should be taken as figurative. Good morals have to do with the love of God and our neighbour, the true faith with our understanding of God and our neighbour." Bray comments, " If the literal sense was unacceptable for some reason, then it was clear to them (the Church Fathers) that God was speaking to his people in another way, and it was up to the interpreter to determine in the light of what he already knew, what that way was." [8]

▶ CHRISTIAN ETHICS IN THE LIGHT OF MODERN BIBLICAL CRITICISM.

Tom Deidun, a Roman Catholic New Testament scholar, has highlighted the relevance of modern critical approaches to the Bible to the subject of Christian Ethics [9]. Deidun mentions the following:

(a) Critics have drawn attention to the diversity of moral teaching throughout the Bible. In the Torah, for instance, moral issues like homosexuality and non-moral subjects like menstruation and touching corpses are not clearly distinguished. In the New Testament also, " ...alongside the small number of fundamental beliefs held in common, there is a considerable diversity of theological and ethical viewpoints."

(b) He believes that the authors of New Testament books have altered events and teaching to suit their purpose (see Oral and Redaction Criticism below). For instance the writer of the Acts of the Apostles records that Peter had the vision of the unclean animals at the very (convenient) time when there was a problem of admitting Gentiles into the church.

(c) Unless we know something about the situations of the original recipients how can we apply the moral teaching to our own situation? For instance was Paul giving his own views about sexual morality in 1 Corinthians chapter 7 or reflecting the views of a spiritual élite group at Corinth, who denigrated the body and imposed an eccentric sexual asceticism that Paul opposed?

(d) The early Christians expected the imminent return of Jesus. Did this influence the way they viewed ethics? For instance did this expectation colour Paul's view about marriage? Was the 'present crisis' (1 Cor.7:27) or the 'time is short' (1 Cor.7:29) a reference to the return of Jesus or some specific trouble?

Modern Biblical Criticism began in the 18th Century. The critical approaches that are relevant to this study are Form Criticism, Redaction Criticism and the more recent approaches of Narrative Criticism, especially in the form of Reader-Response Criticism. Each of these approaches, when properly used, can help find answers to Deidun's questions, but each approach has limitations, and often fails to do justice to the subject as a whole.

Form Criticism is concerned to discover what forms the material that later became the written Bible took in its formative stages. As applied to the Gospels, for example, it concentrates on the oral period between the events of Jesus' life and the final written accounts of his life and teaching in the Gospels. Form critics believe that the original material was passed on in discrete units like parables, miracle stories, and also as legends and myths. Each form was assigned to a specific situation in the life of the early church. It is believed that this oral tradition was added to over the years, a bit like the game Chinese whispers. Scholars cannot agree how much, if any, of the stories and teaching in the Gospels, is authentic material rather than the creation of the early church. This approach makes certain assumptions, which have been challenged. We know that Jews of Jesus' time cultivated memorisation. Some rabbis are known to have memorised the whole of their Bible. We know that the actual words of Jesus were highly prized and were referred to by Paul (e.g. 1 Cor. 11:23-26). Also the time between the death of Jesus and the writing of the gospels was not long enough for legends and myths to develop and throughout this period there were eyewitnesses of the original events who would act as a check on the correctness of what was written. It has also been asked why, if the church made up the teaching of Jesus in response to situations as they arose, that there is no teaching in the gospels to resolve the disputes that took place then. An example of this was whether Gentile converts should be circumcised or should be required to keep the Jewish law.

Redaction Criticism is concerned with the theological assumptions of the writers and how these influenced the way they told the story of Jesus. Each gospel writer had his own agenda and it is important to know what this was. The writers was writing for particular audiences and for particular reasons. Hence they would have selected their sources that suited best their purposes. However, it does not follow that, because they had their own agenda that they were not interested in historical facts.

From the middle of the twentieth century attention has been focussed away from the historical background onto the text itself. Narrative Criticism investigates how the author works out the plot and characterises the action. In a sense this is not new, for interpreters of the gospel stories have frequently drawn attention to the use of hyperbole, irony and paradox in the teaching of Jesus. An example of hyperbole (exaggeration) is Jesus' statement in connection with adultery, " If your right eye causes you to sin, gouge it out and throw it away." (Mt. 5:28) Older commentators also drew attention to the way the writers intend the reader, who knows the end of the story, to interpret the Gospel text in the light of future events. The modern application of this is called Reader-Response Criticism. Whereas Narrative Criticism is concerned with the structure of the text, Reader-Response Criticism focuses on the reader and the reading process. What it means to the Reader becomes the important issue. Hence there is a danger that the reader can read into the text what he wants to find (*eisegesis*) rather than to read from the text what the author intended (*exegesis*).

▶PATRIARCHY AND BIBLICAL ETHICS.

Patriarchy is a term derived from the Latin word for father and is used to describe a hierarchy where the man is dominant in a family relationship. The society represented in the Bible was a patriarchal society. Some biblical critics have argued that the Bible is not a proper guide for Christian ethics because it represents some people as inferior, for instance wives, children and slaves. Adrian Thatcher puts the matter bluntly. " This biblical teaching about marriage is locked into a wider set of assumptions which the biblical writers do not question. The texts show there is a hierarchical order of slave-owners, their wives, their children and their slaves. The head of the household owns the bodies of all the members of it, and rules the household, rather as the emperor rules the empire ... The theology of marriage is so integrated into the institution of slavery and the hierarchical order of social relations which slavery services, that once slavery had been repudiated by Christianity (after nineteen centuries), the theology of marriage based upon it must also be repudiated ... If the teaching on marriage in the New Testament letters is accepted, women are forever to be submissive to men and the same teaching justifies owning slaves." [10]

Thatcher does not do justice to the biblical material. Nowhere does the Bible make a direct comparison between treatment of wives and the treatment of slaves. Certainly Paul urged Christian slaves to submit to their masters, as Peter also urges Christian to submit to the authorities even when they are persecuted (1 Pet.2:13-21). We must see Paul's teaching in the light of his declaration that there is neither slave nor free nor male nor female because they are all one in Christ. He advises slaves to take their freedom if it is offered (1 Cor. 7:21), but realised that if slaves were to revolt against their masters they would come off worse. What Christianity did was to transform the whole concept of master-slave relationships by saying that once someone had become a Christian all barriers of class, race and sex had broken down. In the letter Paul wrote to his Christian friend, Philemon, whose slave had run away to Rome and had become a Christian, Paul tells him to accept him back, " ... no longer as a slave, but better than a slave, as a dear brother." (Philemon verse 16) The same is true with respect to women. When interpreting the passages about submission we need to remember that Christian women were already exercising a freedom unknown in the contemporary Jewish and Graeco-Roman world. Women taught and prophesied in the church and held various offices. It seems that what Paul was trying to prevent was the development of a form of radical feminism that would undermine the whole process of women's liberation. Far from telling husbands to treat their wives like slaves Paul said they were to love their wives as they loved their own bodies and with the self-sacrificial love that Christ had for the Church that he was willing to die for.

Many modern Christian scholars are unhappy with this literal interpretation, and offer alternative ways of applying biblical ethics to modern society. Reader-response critics, for instance, emphasis the importance of a dialogue between the modern reader and the authors of the New Testament letters. In the case of marriage the modern Christian should emphasise equality between husband and wife. Hart draws attention to the irony of a solution which, in order to make the Bible relevant, we need to teach the precise opposite of what it teaches. Other critics, for instance Frances Young, have been more radical. Writing about the Pastoral Letters (1 and 2 Timothy and Titus) she says, " To be true to this perspective (the way the Pastoral Letters deal with specific challenges) requires not the reproduction of the Pastorals' particular ethical maxims so much as a parallel movement to embrace what is universally true and good in the particular social and cultural context in which we find ourselves, while reserving the right to be critical, to jettison value-systems that undermine the moral qualities that are common to decent human life and the gospel." [11]

ARE CHRISTIAN ETHICS RELEVANT TO MODERN SOCIETY?

So far we have considered the Christian approach to ethics and its application to a world that basically accepts the Christian worldview. However, western society has largely abandoned the Christian worldview and its emphasis on absolute ethics in obedience to authoritative teaching. The modern emphasis is largely on seeing ethics as relative and to stress the autonomy of the individual in deciding what is right and wrong. In the light of this, how can Christian ethics have a role to play in modern society? We have seen that two important emphases in New Testament teaching about Christian Ethics are the importance of love and of living a life of holiness. There are two ethical theories that focus on these, namely Situation Ethics and Virtue Ethics.

▶ **CHRISTIAN ETHICS AS LOVE - SITUATION ETHICS.**

Jesus taught that the most important commandment was to love God and our neighbour and Paul spoke of the most excellent way as being the way of love. If this is the case, couldn't Christian ethics be simply expressed as following the path of love. The American theologian and moralist, Joseph Fletcher and a former English bishop and theologian, John Robinson, advocated an ethical philosophy in which the only thing that matters in making moral decisions is whether it is the loving thing to do. There is nothing that is intrinsically right or wrong, but everything must be judged according to circumstances. The only intrinsic good is love, which Fletcher said was the same as justice, because justice means giving to other people their due and what is due to them is love. When making ethical decisions we are not bound by law but each decision must be made in the light of foreseeable consequences. This means that acts which are generally regarded as wrong such as abortion, infanticide, adultery and even murder, may in certain circumstances be right and justified if they are motivated by love. Can situation ethics be considered a form of Christian ethics? The following should be considered in our evaluation of it:

(a) It is right to insist that the New Testament teaches that only by loving and caring for others can we rightly serve God (see Rom. 13:8-10)

(b) Situation Ethics provide a corrective to the legalism that Jesus criticised, which put obedience to legal principles above concern for the individual.

(c) It is right to emphasise the uniqueness of each situation and therefore exercise flexibility in seeking to follow a path that is best for all concerned.

Yet:-

(d) It is not always possible to know what the outcome of our actions will be.

(e) Love is often blind (for instance it can come from the emotions and not from reason) and can lead to wrong decisions being taken.

(f) The Bible insists that we love God **by keeping his commandments**. (John 14:15f; 1 John 5:3)

(g) Even when we are forced to make a choice of moral principles (the lesser of two evils), such as stealing to feed a starving person, the act is still morally wrong.

▶ LIVING THE GOOD LIFE - VIRTUE ETHICS.

Elizabeth Anscombe, as we noted at the beginning of this booklet, pointed out that modern philosophy has no ultimate justification for why we should act morally. She sought that justification in virtue ethics. This ethical theory is concerned less with what ought to be done, and more on what makes a person moral. Christianity stresses the importance of living a virtuous life and of being an example to others. The guiding ethical principles were love, service and humility.

Virtue Ethics was rooted in the classical world of the New Testament and is particularly associated with Aristotle. He maintained that everyone wants to live the good life. In order to do this we must be able to exist alongside other people, giving due regard to their interests. To achieve this we must cultivate a stable disposition whereby we react appropriately to particular situations. Aristotle believed the virtuous person follows the middle course between extremes. His definition of a courageous person would be someone who acts reasonably and not recklessly by taking into consideration any risks involved. He defined vices as the extremes, for instance foolhardiness and cowardice and virtue as the 'golden mean' which, in our example, would be courage. The moral person is one who learns from the example of others rather than by following a set of rules.

Christian teachers, like Augustine, criticised Aristotle because he believed pagan virtues and vices were expressions of human pride and did not come from the knowledge of the true God. For him all virtues are expressions of God's love. Aquinas, who had a greater sympathy for Aristotle, distinguished between virtues bestowed upon us by God without any action on our part and those acquired by us through rational reflection. In more modern times Friedrich Schleiermacher (1768-1834) based his analysis of the Christian religion on the awareness of the Infinite and absolute dependence on divine reality, which included a belief in the highest good. His ethical system was heavily dependent on Aristotle.

In what way can Virtue Ethics be seen as an expression of Christian Ethics? It is a system that readily adapts to our pluralistic and relativistic society because it can be all things to all men. It can reflect the 'middle way' of Buddhism, the tenets of Humanism as well as reflecting some important aspects of Christianity. It can be easily understood, is not unrealistic and can be applied to the whole of humanity. Nevertheless it can be criticised:

   (a) Virtue Ethics seeks to separate ethics from rules, but without rules it would be impossible to judge whether someone is virtuous.

   (b) The virtuous person, according to this scheme, can be like the Pharisees whom Jesus criticised. Virtue ethics can encourage someone to follow a course of action to win praise from others rather than to help people out of genuine concern for them.

(c) Virtue is culturally dependent. What might be considered virtuous in one culture, like committing suicide for a cause (e.g. suicide bombings or a widow throwing herself on the funeral pyre of her husband) may be considered a sin in another.

(d) Virtue ethics may not be able to help in specific moral dilemmas. An example, which has been discussed, is that of a pregnant mother with a severely deformed foetus. How could she decide between following the mean of 'being brave or compassionate' or of 'being pragmatic'?

There are those who would criticise both Virtue Ethics and Christian Ethics for failing to make ethics work in society. The philosopher Richard Taylor (Ethics, Faith and Reason:1985) claims that Christianity is wrong to teach an equality in which the poor, the weak, the ignorant and stupid are promised treasures in Heaven because this discourages people from putting in the effort to become stronger and nobler. For him pride in ones achievements is a virtue, not a vice. Taylor has highlighted the difference between Christian ethics and much modern thought and, at the same time, shown a misunderstanding of Christianity. Christianity teaches that all people have the same intrinsic value as creatures made in the image of God, but not necessarily having the same moral worth. Jesus condemned those who were proud, self-centred, hypocritical or greedy. He commended those who were generous and humble and encouraged people to strive, with God's help, to become virtuous. It is this emphasis that makes Christian Ethics important and relevant to the modern world.

REFERENCES

[1] Anscombe. Essay reprinted in *Virtue Ethics*. Ed. Roger Crisp and Michael Slote (Oxford University Press 1997) p31

[2] Jones in *The Cambridge Companion to Christian Ethics*. Ed. Robin Gill (Cambridge University Press 2001) p17

[3] Klausner. *Jesus of Nazareth: His Life, Times and Teaching*. (London. Allen and Unwin 1929) p384.

[4] Hart. *The Ethics of Jesus*. (Cambridge Grove Books 1997) p11.

[5] MacLeod in *The Trustworthiness of God*. Ed. Paul Helm and Carl Trueman. (Leicester Apollos 2002) p72

[6] White *Biblical Ethics*. (Exeter. Paternoster 1979) p60.

[7] White. Op.cit. p88.

[8] Bray (ref.5) p163

[9] Deidun in *Christian Ethics: An Introduction*. Ed. Bernard Hoose (London Cassell 1998) p4-20.

[10] Thatcher. *Liberating Se*. (London SPCK. 1993) p16

[11] Young. *The Theology of the Pastoral Letters*. (Cambridge University Press 1994) p153

WORKSHEET

1. How might each of the following be applied by a Christian to help solve ethical dilemmas?

    (a) The Bible

    (b) Christian Tradition

    (c) Conscience

    (d) Situation Ethics

    (e) Virtue Ethics

2. Outline with illustrations the advantages and disadvantages of basing Christian Ethics on obedience to God's commandments.

3. What is meant by the "Euthyphro Dilemma" and how might it apply to Christian Ethics?

4. What is meant by the term "natural law" and explain the role of Natural Law in Christian Ethics.

5. In what ways did the ethical teaching of Jesus differ from the teaching of the Jewish Bible (Old Testament)?

6. How important is modern Biblical Criticism in determining the way the Bible is to be used in Christian Ethics?

EXAM QUESTION

Exam questions on ethics tend to focus on one particular issue/area, such as environment or abortion. It sounds obvious but the most important thing to do is to answer the question. One way of attempting to do this is at the end of writing each paragraph ask the question, "What has this got to do with the title?". Once you have thought about this write it at the end of the paragraph, so that the examiner is clear how the question has been answered.

It is also very important to plan your essay. This will help give you the necessary structure in order to answer the question. Consider the following example:

"The New Testament teaching about marriage is irrelevant to modern day Christians since it is based on an outdated view of hierarchy portraying the husband as the head of the household."

Explain and assess this assertion.

The **explanation** part of the answer involves an unpackaging of the assertion. First the evidence from the New Testament would have to be given, supporting the view that the husband was considered head of the family. Then the explanation as to why the husband, if regarded as head of the household, shows a hierarchical view. Further, it would be necessary to argue how this hierarchical approach to society was not one that represented present western society. Hence a view using such an approach must be considered irrelevant. Given the New Testament seems to reflect this approach, the New Testament must be considered irrelevant.

Assessment will involve putting forward arguments that support and challenge that view and conclusion. For instance some debate about the authority of the Bible as a guide to morals would need to be discussed. It could also be challenged as to what the Bible does say about the role and position of the husband. For instance, Biblical criticism could raise issues about whether the Early Christians expected the imminent return of Jesus and whether this influenced their ethical teaching (interim ethics, which are not valid for all time). Likewise Reader-Response criticism – how do we bring our situation to bear on the interpretation of the Bible? Should we see Bible teaching as a merely human response to divine revelation that must be updated continually through the insights of Church leaders, theologians and moral philosophers?

Conclusion: Maybe there isn't a clear-cut conclusion. However it is vital that your conclusion, whatever it is, has been supported by the body of your answer.

FURTHER READING

The Puzzle of Ethics.
By Peter Vardy and Paul Grosch. (Fount Rev.Ed. 1999)
Readability *** Content ###
A very good and thorough introduction to ethical theories and their application. Part 1 is particularly applicable, especially the sections on Kant, Situation Ethics, Natural Law and Virtue Ethics.

Foundations for the Study of Religion.
By Libby Ahluwalia (Hodder and Stoughton 2001)
Readability **** Content ####
A comprehensive volume especially written for A Level. Chapters 1,2 and 5 are particularly relevant.

The Cambridge Companion to Christian Ethics.
Editor Robin Gill. (Cambridge University Press 2001)
Readability ** Content ####
A series of essays written by experts in their field. It is comprehensive in its scope. I particularly recommend the chapters on Biblical Ethics, Natural Law and Virtue Ethics.

Christian Ethics: An Introduction.
Editor Bernard Hoose (Cassell 1998)
Readability *** Content #
This book covers the same ground as the Cambridge Companion but from a Roman Catholic perspective. The contributions are varied and not up to the standard of the Cambridge volume.

Grove Booklets (Ridley Hall, Cambridge)
Readability *** Content ###
Grove Publication have produced a very good series of booklets relevant to Christian Ethics. The following are particularly recommended.

The Ethics of Jesus. Colin Hart (1997)

The Ethics of the Gospels. Colin Hart (1998)

The Ethics of Paul. Colin Hart (1999)

The Ethics of the Later Pauline Letters. Colin Hart. (2000)

The Ethics of the Letter of James. Greg. Forster. (2002)

Scripture and Authority Today. John Bauckham (1999)

A Slippery Slope? R. T. France (2000)
France's booklet is particularly helpful in relating specific New Testament teaching to modern situations.

KEY Readability   * manageable;   ** good;
    *** very good;   **** excellent.

Content   # adequate;   ## good;
    ### very good;   #### excellent.

NOTES